The Comfort of Crows
Denise Neita - Chen

This work of poetry is based on events and observations in the poet's experiences. Some events are based on real people and events, whereas others are the product of the poet's imagination.

Denise Neita-Chen
9 Surbiton Road
Kingston 10
Jamaica. W.I.

As a poet, I have had too many Brother Gilbert from the film *Dragonheart* moments; 'Oh that was good, what did I say? What did I say?'

THE COMFORT OF CROWS

List of poems

THE COMFORT OF CROWS

Despair

Despair eats at the soul like a slow moving cancer
It robs all of life
Of hope
Of truth
Despair is a bitter pill
Forced down the throat of the hopeless
Of the helpless
Of the meek
Despair weighs around the neck
Like the millstone of a suicide
Of a screaming child
Of the bereaved wife
Despair eats away
Erodes away
Empties all
Until only normal is left
Hopeless
Colourless
Rootless
Lifeless
Only to exist in sorrow.
Jan. 15, 2015.

DENISE NEITA-CHEN

The Comfort Of Crows

Black shiny glossed coats
Black yet clear eyes
The great cawing noise
Living in trees and calling
Carrion eaters who like death
Associated with the grim reaper
A shoulder to perch
In the other hand a sickle
Calling in the wind
Dancing in the trees
An eerie but beautiful sight
To see them perched
But death omens they are
They smell death
They see it
They call to it
I stand here and watch
I see the death van exit
All that is left
Is the comfort of crows
February 21, 2015

THE COMFORT OF CROWS

Footsteps

I was not there when those footsteps
Brought you home from the hospital
I didn't see the smiles on your parents faces
That was before I was born
But I saw you as a child bustling in the kitchen
I was underfoot dogging your steps
You were beautiful to me
Laughing with joy, always beautiful to me
I was there at your wedding
Watching you walk down the aisle
Dancing at your reception
Even though at seven, I was more fascinated by the drink fountain
I was there for dinners and Christmases
When your steps were slower
When infirmity took its toll
When you burial your mother
Then there was that fateful day
I watched as those men came
I followed their steps as they carried you out
I watched as they put in you
I followed as the van disappeared
I closed the gates
Those gates that you would never step through anymore
I turned and my steps were hollow
I saw my brother standing just as bereft
Your footsteps for us to follow no more.

March 4, 2015
for Aunt Vivienne (June 21,1951 - June 24, 2013)

DENISE NEITA-CHEN

An obedient child

I have always been an obedient child
Doing what my God has told me
I have been molested
Raped
Vilified
And humiliated
But I have been an obedient child
I have always been an obedient child
Doing what my God has told me
While I have been persecuted
Lied to
Had insults hurled at
Beaten
Mocked
And been lied about
But I have been an obedient child
I have always been an obedient child
Doing what my God has told me
While I cowered in fear
From men with guns
That spit fire and death
Amidst the screams of my fellow children
But I have been an obedient child
I have always been an obedient child
Doing what my God has told me
While I held in my arms a baby
Who would die in a hail of bullets
Meant for someone else
While I held the hand of a child
Whose life has fallen apart

THE COMFORT OF CROWS

Because her parents have chosen divorce
And through this I have been an obedient child
I have always been an obedient child
Doing what my God has told me
Even when I railed in the night
Against the injustices that I suffered
When I was forced to wear the shame
Of my attackers
When I felt alone, desolate and abandoned
Still I was an obedient child
I have shown my enemies compassion and kindness
I have been generous to the ungrateful
I have taught love
When my students responded with hate
I have shed my tears and my blood
I have sacrificed myself
I have laid down my life for strangers
All this I have done
For I am an obedient child
Doing what my God has asked me.

December 18, 2015

Mirror

I look in the mirror
I hate what I see
The eyes
The nose
The lips
Times three
I look in the mirror
I hate what I see
My hair
My skin
My waist
Times three
I look in the mirror
I hate what I see
The lines
Of lies
Anger and time
I look in the mirror
I hate what I see
A person
A woman
That is
Me
May 5, 2016

THE COMFORT OF CROWS

Words

Words that strangle and can not come out
The words that are vomited from my soul
And can not be heard
I can not speak
I feel twisted inside
Like pretzels tossed in the wind
Pressure builds on all sides
All I do is cry
And I do not cry
Words are to give life
Give breath
Give memory
All I feel is a cacophony of noise
I can not be heard
I scream
I shout
I cry
And I do not cry
My chest feels like an elephant
That sits on it
Crushing all sound
Crushing all life
These are words that are vomited from my soul
Who will hear them?
Who will care?
My failures are reminders
Of the impotence of my words
Of my feelings
Of my needs
I spend so much time crying

And I do not cry.
My soul is dying
My life is meaningless
I scream
But there is no sound
I cry
I shout
These are the things that are vomited from my soul
Who will hear?
Who will care?
November 2, 2016

THE COMFORT OF CROWS

The Path Not Taken

I often sit and ponder about the other paths
That have merged and joined with mine
Ones that would have led to other places
Was I at one point like the character
In the Frost poem, looking down the road
That forked in the forest?
Was I, like that man who had to choose
Whether to go the way of everyone else,
Or the way very few have tread?
Was it bravery or cowardice?
Or worse indifference?
I look back at my life
I look back at the path I wandered down.
(I have to say wandered down, because I didn't choose.)
And I see what other choices I could have made.
I could have been wife and mother,
(But what would have happened to those I nurtured?)
I could have held a job with a huge salary
(But what of those I saved from despair and destruction?)
I could have had all the things money could buy:
Fame, fortune and all the rest.
(But what of the empty-eyed children who never would have had hope?)
What is this path that I have taken?
It is one that has caused me grief and suffering,
(But kept me from the fists of at least two men)
It has made me childless
(Though there are many times my womb has leapt for joy that it is
barren)
It has made me the keeper of knowledge.
(A lot of secrets I wish I could un-know.)

This path that I wandered down,
(How silly a girl I was)
Is not a path for the faint of heart.
It is filled with pitfalls and potholes
(A thing I have never seen my country's roads without)
But now at almost the midpoint
I finally understand Macbeth,
One must go to the other side
(Despite being a strong swimmer I would drown)
What is it Frost said?
The path chosen made all the difference?
At the end of my life
My tombstone shall not read
She went the way of others
Instead it should say:
In the end she made a difference, changing lives and the world.
(But that is probably a vain hope.)
A result of the path that I wandered down, merrily and happily,
Encompassing demise, salvation or both.
March 25, 2017

THE COMFORT OF CROWS

A Tale of Two Fathers

Like so many in our modern society
I have never lived with the man
Who made my mother pregnant.
That man was named Kenneth.
He was a handsome man,
What many would call a 'sweet mout' bwoy.
He had a woman in every town,
Spread his seed far and wide
Uncaring of the result until pressed.
He treated my mother like all the rest,
Shamefully and abominably.
Like so many before her,
She was humiliated.
He embarrassed her when she went to ask for money,
She needed to go to the doctor.
She was pregnant with me.
Her sister, Aunt Norma intervened.
She went with her tiny four feet nine inch self,
She got the money from him
She was upset.
She spoke with Aunt Claire,
My mother's other sister.
They banded together.
They protected my mother.
They were there when I was born.
At first he visited,
Kenneth taking me to where he worked to show-off
The light skinned baby with straight hair.
Then my mother decided that she had ambitions for me
As only a child of an industrious woman would.

But Kenneth was no help.
So, with her sisters and the rest of the family, they bid him goodbye.
He left gladly
A burden (me) lifted.
Later in my life
When because of my curiosity
My mother found him
He said that he remembered the relationship but
Not that there was a child.
Which brings me to Howard.
My daddy. The only man I have ever called that.
I was still a baby, when he met my mother.
He said that she was feisty
He liked her
He was not a man for responsibility
But accepted that she had a child.
Then began my earliest memories.
This man, who was always strong,
Carrying me everywhere
I was his daughter.
His parents were my other grandparents.
Even though I called them uncle and aunt
It didn't matter.
His sisters Vivienne and Debbie
My aunts too.
I was an accepting child
I didn't question
It was my reality.
When I was sick
My daddy was there
When I am ill
My daddy is still there.

THE COMFORT OF CROWS

All my life this man has been my rock.
He has held my hand
He has loved my mother
He gave me my brother Sheldon.
He once said that my mother
Was the sun for us.
Our lives revolved around her
But he has always been that rock. That steady hand.
That iron grip.
He saw me through a lot.
He has stood proudly at graduations
He was pale and white-skinned
When I was in hospital
He has sat in doctors' offices
In hospitals
In car parks
He is not perfect
For no man is.
But for all his faults, they are easily outweighed by his quiet strength.
He has held my mother's hand
Through all their marriage vows
Yes, they bicker now.
But it is with amusement that others see.
A cute old couple walking hand in hand down the street.
As for that other man,
What is it to be told?
I asked him once for help
He said that he would call me back on Monday
That Monday never came
My daddy, Howard, is the one who was there
When a metal stand tried to part my skull
Through the doctors, tests and lawyer too.

When everything has gone wrong and I can barely move
It is my daddy who comes to soothe.
I look back and I think
There was God's hand
In these things.
He helped my aunts chase Kenneth away,
So that my daddy Howard would come to stay.
For who else could have known
What to do with a strange little child
Who sat in a corner
And watched as life ran by.
Who else would could have discussed philosophy
When a little girl discovered mythology?
My daddy is a quiet man.
A strong man.
An ordinary man,
Who took up the mantle that was cast aside,
And made that little child into the poet
I am inside.

April 11, 2017

Carlton, the Taxi-man

When I was a little girl,
My mother met a Taxi-man.
He drove a yellow and black
Checkered coloured cab.
(But my mother says it was yellow.)
He was slim,
Black,

THE COMFORT OF CROWS

Soft-spoken,
And gentle.
He took my mother where
She needed to go
Then they came to an arrangement
As it was often done in those days,
She hired him to take me to school.
I was a small child,
But I had been trained to be polite,
"Good morning, Carlton."
"Thank you, Carlton."
"Have a nice day, Carlton."
And so it went,
Me, a small child,
Riding in the backseat of the cab.
With my mother in the mornings,
By myself in the afternoons.
It became a habit,
A pattern,
A steady routine.
"Good afternoon, Carlton."
"Thank you, Carlton."
"Goodbye, and see you tomorrow, Carlton."
Perhaps he was amused,
Driving a little girl,
Whose feet could not even touch the floor.
For after a while, I became accustomed.
Thus with a child's innocence,
I began to talk.
On the journey home,
Every day,
Carlton would be regaled.

There were many stories that had to be told.
I wonder if his ears ever burned?
But not once did he silence me,
Just let me chatter on,
Giving confidence in a quiet way.

One day my mother tells the tale,
Carlton turned up after school, late.
He had had a fare,
It took him long,
An irate me,
Did not understand.
I sat in the back,
Quiet as can be,
Then finally said
In a very firm tone.
"Carlton, if you are late again, I shall walk home!"
Of course, that was an idle threat,
At that age,
I had no idea how to get home.
But I was a serious little child,
And while my mother laughed,
Carlton feared my determined little mind.
He told his employers,
He could not take the chance,
The little girl had to come first.
Never again was he late.
But then as Fate would have it,
There was another day.
Carlton had a fare, my mother said,
He told the woman,
He had a stop

THE COMFORT OF CROWS

To make.
He told her, she had to sit in front.
No one could sit next to the little girl.
He picked me up,
With the stranger in the car,
I was polite, and quiet for the whole ride.
To Harbour View we drove.
He thought a treat for a little child.
When he had deposited his fare,
And was on the way to drop me home,
I said quietly, "Carlton, when you pick me up, you are to take me directly
home."
He said for the rest of the ride
I was quiet.
He told my mother,
He was amazed,
I waited till after
The fare had paid
And we were on our way.
Then, there came a day,
When I was with the others in the School,
We played in the front yard.
A man came down the street
Wearing just a cloth around his waist
Everything about him on display.
The little boys stared and compared,
Then the man's shouts rent the air.
The others scampered off and ran
I followed them as I also ran.
But the man's words stayed with me,
Until the need to know overcame me.
I reached forward to the bench seat

And meekly asked,
"Carlton, what does bomboclaat mean?"
His hand came off the steering wheel,
His head spun towards me and back to the street.
"Child, where you hear dat word?"
"From a mad-man in front of the School," I replied.
"Child, don't repeat what mad-man say," he admonished.
He continued driving staring ahead,
"Don't say dat word and let your mother hear, next thing you know,
she think I cuss bad-word in front of you."
I sat back and remained quiet,
In fact, I only told my mother that story just yesterday.
Then came the time they broke into our house.
Carlton was about to drop me off.
He frowned and stared at the house for a while.
"Child get down on the floor and remain quiet," his voice was stern,
It was a tone I had never heard. "If you hear me yell run," he continued,
"open the door, and run next door."
Then from under his seat he withdrew the biggest machete I had ever
seen.
But I obeyed and remained on the floor.
Then he returned.
He took me next door.
Asked the lady to look after me.
The house had been broken into.
He went for my mother and the police.
We moved after that.
My mother refuses to live in a house with a lot of land.
Carlton continued to drive me,
Until my mother learned to drive
She bought a car
We did not need Carlton any more.

THE COMFORT OF CROWS

I can't remember if I got the chance to tell him goodbye. I hope I did.

There came the elections of 1980
A bloody event in our nation's history.
We heard on the news,
A man was set upon by a mob,
Beaten to death
Dragged behind the Politician led march,
His body dumped on
The steps of Police High Commission
Like refuse.
I heard and was saddened.
But we didn't know,
Until a few years later
Who it was.
It was Carlton, the Taxi-man,
His brother also drove a taxi, and was an activist.
They mistook Carlton for him.
They rained blows,
They took his life,
Never once did he say they were not right.
They desecrated him, by dragging his body around,
Those who took part in the slaughter of this innocent man.
Carlton, the Taxi-man,
How much he missed.
He had the care of a precocious child,
Quiet care he took.
He was a good man,
Who never deserved the fate that occurred.

May 5, 2017

DENISE NEITA-CHEN

Invigilation
Time ticks slowly by,
It is amazing how long
Five minutes seem like an hour
When you are bored out of your mind.
For the students, (well those who are prepared)
An hour passes far too quickly.
Heads bowed scratching responses on paper
Will they be rewarded?
Will they be failed?
Well that is up to the markers.
Those people who sit up in the night,
With babies on their bed,
Grading the illegible scribbles.
Attempting to decipher the symbols drawn
All in the name of giving a grade.
Of course there are rules to be followed.
Watch them so they do not cheat,
Though they are creative
When they decide to and not often are they caught.
Grade the papers to a certain scale,
Though you know they should fail.
Meeting quotas and standards,
But at the end of it all,
What purpose does it serve?
Like a hamster on the wheel,
Round and round.
These grades or marks
What differences abound?
Degrees and other papers,
What does it truly mean?
What purpose? What use are these?

THE COMFORT OF CROWS

Our children rack their brains,
Fill themselves up with facts and names.
But will they truly find their purpose just the same?
When the doctor has finished studying,
What shall he or she do, when it is discovered medicine is a guessing game?
Experiments and tests are done,
But we cannot stop a simple cold.
We cannot address the real ailments
So in the end
What use is the study?
As I sit here looking at these girls,
Scratching away on various papers,
I do wonder
What purpose does all this serve?

June 29, 2017

It's all my mother's fault
I sit here
A product of my mother.
She conceived me in the womb,
Grew me with her body,
Birthed me into this world,
Brought me into a family
And it's all my mother's fault.
It is my mother's fault
That I can read
For she insisted that it was important.
It is my mother's fault that
I am educated
She pushed me out the door everyday
Without fail.
I attended, nursery, preparatory school, high school
And University.
She still laments I didn't just finish everything and get that
Pesky Ph.D
I could have been a doctor of letters
I could have been a lawyer
Instead I became a teacher.
Someone who looks at recalcitrant girls
And drags them kicking and screaming
Towards a sound education.
That too is mother's fault
She taught me to be compassionate and kind
Then turns around and rages
When I am taken advantaged of.
But it's a difficult line to walk.
However that too is my mother's fault.
My mother insisted that I be self-sufficient

THE COMFORT OF CROWS

Depend on myself for my own way in the world
Not to expect some man to take care of me.
Be at no man's mercy
Yet has regretted that I took her too literally,
No grandchildren at her feet.
She did say when I was in my teens
She didn't want to be called grandma.
If some find me complicated
That is her fault too,
She encouraged me to develop a voracious appetite for knowledge
Encouraged the knowing and understanding of things.
But it makes me intimidating
Complex
Funny
Not the kind of woman a man wants to marry.
Do I regret the way things turned out?
No, not at all.
I'm perfectly happy
In my own imperfect way
I love the days that go by
Especially when it rains
I like what I like
I'm just fine
And that too is all my mother's fault.
July 29, 2017

DENISE NEITA-CHEN

We in the Caribbean

We in the Caribbean live our lives
At Nature's whim and fancy
We dread that season from
June to November
Why?
It is the hurricane season
The thunderstorms leave the African continent
And traverse that same route
As the middle passage
Encountering those souls lost along the way
Growing in might
Seething with rage for things done
So many centuries ago.
Hurtling across the salt water
Building up in circles
Until an eye is formed
That centre which remains calm
While all around it the wind howls and shrieks
Finally coming ashore and laying waste
To all things for those descendants of slaves
To those descendants of slavers
Indentured
Freed
Tricked
Exiled
We in the Caribbean live our lives by the sea
These small islands
That seep with our blood
Our sweat
Our tears

THE COMFORT OF CROWS

Every year, we pray
Let no storms come
All times we get an answer
Just that sometimes it's no.

September 18, 2017

Sunday Sermon
What is conscience?
What is salvation?
I sit here listening to the Archbishop drone on...
It is a cool morning
The sun has come out
Yet here we are sitting in a building
Listening to the Archbishop drone on
About
Forgiveness
Light
Jesus
We must pray
For
Wisdom
Strength
Grace
And mercy'
The Archbishop drones on
Drives on
Not realising that we are tired
We are praying
For
Salvation
Light
Forgiveness

And mercy
November 12, 2017

THE COMFORT OF CROWS

Today I saw Juliana with a black eye,
I was shocked and horrified
It is not as though she is someone I like,
In fact quite the opposite
She is someone I have always detested.
It's odd to me, for my cousin has the same name,
But we do not call her that,
For which I'm thankful
For my cousin I love quite well.
But back to Juliana and her black eye,
She is a horrid person, always the same,
She has her children
Dirty, noisy and straggling
They are never quiet
Well, there was that one time,
She had sat in the same church pew
For the whole mass,
They made not a peep
I was most cross faced, indeed.
Yet it is true that with Christian values,
We are to be kind and generous
Even though she does push me to the limit.
I spoke once to the priest,
He dismissed my concerns as a case of her incapable of mothering.
So many children she has hanging on her skirt-tail
That no one knows quite what to do.
She punched one once
I grabbed the child from her
And had harsh words
She has not done that at church since

But I come back to Juliana's black eye
A thing that triggers bad memories inside
A memory of my mom's friend aunt Jean
On a dark night
Going to her ex's house
We waited in the car
There were screams and shouts
It was very loud
She ran back to the car
Drove us away
Her face was cut
Blood from a glass shard
I didn't know what to say
I was so young when I heard
But inside it made me burn
Later, a year or two
There was my namesake
Denise
She was bright and beautiful
Worked as a secretary
For my mom's boss
Aunt Mary
I was always amazed at the typing.
Then there was the fact
That she was my babysitter
She was pretty and fun
We went swimming and everything
Until the day she fell in love.
Louis was his name
He was a medical student
Realised that my spine was curved
But there was something about him

THE COMFORT OF CROWS

I never liked
Then one day after school
I walked to my mother's workplace
There was Denise, wearing sunglasses
It was inside and it was strange
I ran into Aunt Mary's office
I asked her why Denise was wearing sunglasses inside
Aunt Mary who always smoked
Had her cigarette in its long holder
Her eyes narrowed
She said to stay there
Then called Denise inside.
"Take off the sunglasses," Aunt Mary said.
Denise complied.
There over her eye was a big black and blue bruise
Her eye was swollen and watery
"What happened?" Aunt Mary demanded.
"I walked into a door," was the reply.
Aunt Mary huffed, "That looks more like you walked into a fist!"
Denise remained silent.
Aunt Mary dismissed her back to her desk.
She turned to me, still holding the cigarette tightly,
"Never let any man do that to you," she admonished.
I nodded dumbly.

Denise was a person I loved,
She did not heed the warnings,
Married Louis,
Bore him a daughter named Natalie,
Continued to be beaten by Louis
Until one day he smashed her head into a wall
Cracked her skull

She had had enough
She grabbed the kettle and fought back
Dented the metal against his head
Divorced him
Fought him and won alimony
Managed to get her life on track
A good tale,
Except she was still the same
A pretty woman
Very little brain
She met another fellow
Leo was his name.
Leo treated her well
Did his best to heal her
But him I trusted less the same.
I felt there was something oily about him
A darkness that my mother dismissed
Saying I was just suspicious.
Then came the news,
Leo was a bad person
A Columbian drug dealer
Those people you heard of to be feared
Cocaine was where his money came from
But he was low level

He tried to steal money from Louis
Louis was upset
He was willing to forgive
But Denise had to leave Leo
Or lose Natalie
Leo then did the terrible thing
Hired thugs

THE COMFORT OF CROWS

Who were paid to kill.
They beat Louis
Drowned him in his bathtub
A horrible death

Then came the worse
Denise was caught up in this curse
Leo escaped, ran back to Columbia
(I sincerely hope he is rotting away in some jungle down there)
As for Denise
The police didn't believe she was innocent
That Louis was worth more to her alive than dead
Even the killers said
She was innocent
The District Attorney didn't care
She had to be guilty
The money trail led to her
Leo, the coward was clever
Made sure it didn't touch him
Left a baby in her belly
For good measure
Natalie an orphan too
Father dead
Mother jailed
She's still in there to this day.
Natalie was raised by her father's parents
Taught to hate her mother
The other child
Raised by her mother's father
Denise's mother disowned her
She loved Louis more than her.
All these things ran in my head

Triggered by the sight of Juliana and her black eye
Also in my head was Susan
A silly girl
Very pretty
Girlfriend to Cecil
Who we pitied
His sister took their father's gun
Shot herself by the pool
Cecil was disturbed
That much was true
He beat Susan
And we were teens
We got her to leave him
Good that seemed
But one night in the club
Cecil he brought his father's gun
But he didn't count on the other boys
Who grabbed him and led him away
Susan became quiet after that
She needed care
I don't know how well she fared
But these were the things that travelled
Through my head
Violence against women
Maybe violence against men?
I looked at Rose,
Juliana's mother
I said, 'Who gave her the black eye?'
Rose shook her head
'Her **gentle-man**,' she said.
I looked at Rose puzzled,
'You would stand for that?' I asked

THE COMFORT OF CROWS

Rose shook her head 'no' in reply.
'She will not listen to reason I suppose,' I too shook my head.
'She's a grown woman and mother of her children,' Rose said as she shrugged.
But I know that code,
It meant that Rose has quarreled with her daughter
Until she has given up,
Juliana will not listen
I know that type
They will continue
Until there is nothing left,
Except perhaps death.
Juliana hid her head from me,
She saw the rage in my eyes
When I saw her black eye.
A woman I truly detest,
But not someone who I had not wished the best.
I have wanted her to take control
Be the mother, her brood deserves.
But that black eye reminds me of the rest,
And I remember I should not be put to the test.
All these things had occurred,
Because I saw Juliana with
That black eye of hers.
November 12-15, 2017

DENISE NEITA-CHEN

A Grecian Poet in Rome

(For Ramona O'Meally, who gave me this message from God. Never let anyone
make you feel, anything other than what you are, a beloved child of God.)

I am and have always been a faithful servant
Of God,
But,
If I had known then, what I know now,
I would go back in time and pluck out my eyes,
For being blinded I would then be free to actually see.
I would also go back and stop up my ears,
For being deaf I would then be able to hear
The words of my Lord,
And not be confused by cries of others
I would peel off my skin
So that I would not feel the
Flays of barbed whips and tongues,
I would not feel,
The wounds made by swords of misdeeds and evil.
I would then by being blind and deaf to the world
Know that every scar I carry
Is also carried by God.
That as they have whipped me and spat on me in the streets,
They hurt Christ upon the cross.
That every nail they wounded me with,
Caused Him to bleed and feel pain.
I by being blind and deaf would fulfil the tasks set to me.
I would serve as a beacon of hope, love and forgiveness.
I would by my prayers

Bring the pain of God's people closer to His Ear.
I would serve my task,
I would save their souls.
May 16, 2019

If I am done in

If I am done in,
It shall be at my cat's paws
For she rightly believes that I have done her wrong.
If I am done in,
It shall be at my cat's paws
For I dared to give her a bath, that's all.
If I am done in,
It shall be at my cat's paws
For how dare I shampoo her of all the dirt that's hers!
It is wrong! that's her view of it all.
If I am done in,
It shall be at my cat's paws
For she sits looking at me evilly from beside the wall,
As she licks her paws and sharpens her claws.

If I am done in,
It shall be at my cat's paws
For sixteen years of vet visits, exams and more,
After all, I take her to be weighed and violated, as well as blood drawn.

If I am done in,
It shall be at my cat's paws
For she plots revenge for all the wrong I have done her,
Although I do claim to love her, but she sees the effect,
Not that it matters
As long as my scars are scattered.
May 6, 2022.

THE COMFORT OF CROWS

Come

Come,
Let us go down to
St. Joseph's
The hospital that houses the cancer unit.
Come,
Let us see the
Machine
The one that makes the patient irradiated.
Come,
Let us sit in
The room
While waiting for the nurse to call.
Come
Let us be poked
And prodded
Measured and weighed as we wait to be called again.
Come,
Let us undress
Into gowns
To be laid upon the table, clothed yet bare.
Come,
While we wait
Our turn
Watching as others take theirs in turn.
Come,
Let us talk awhile
About
Our ordinary lives
Come,
Let us speak

Of the present and the past
As we wait while the time passes by.
Come,
As we take
Our books
For the next appointment time
See,
All these people,
Young, old and in-between
Joined together by one disease.
Learn,
Their stories
As well as their names
For sickness has no manners
Treats all the same.
Oct. 28, 2022

THE COMFORT OF CROWS

I watched
I stood there and watched as my brother
knelt on the neck of his brother
as the brother pleaded and begged.
I watched as my sisters' voices cried out loud
begging our brother not to kill
his own brother.
I saw the thousands gathered in the streets protesting
rioting and looting
I saw anger and hate.
I sat huddled in the corner as my children lit places on fire
threw grenades and fired guns
all while ignoring my pleas to stop.
I cried as thousands have continued to die,
through this endless war
of blooding running in the streets.
I watched as my grandchild picked up shards of glass
trying with tiny hands
to fix what went wrong.
I walked as others threw bottles at me
while cowards behind desks
signed papers to end women's healthcare.
I listened as my aunts and uncles turned
against my grandparents
and their own children.
I heard the missiles thundering in the air
while my daughter lay labouring
to bring new life into the world.
I see people standing up against tyrants
being beaten savagely into the ground
while soldiers threaten and pillage.
I look into the distance and see my

God with tears on His face
begging His children to love each other.
May 1, 2023

The Sorrow Prayer

As I sit here in this darkened room,
The windows are painted black.
Flashes come before me
Without colour,
Without light.
As the desperate claws of sorrow
Tear at me like nails grating
Against the chalkboard
I am alone.
This was how it was in the beginning
And ever shall be
World without end
Amen.

THE COMFORT OF CROWS

Schemes

I often wonder why teachers call their lesson plans schemes
It brings to mind the vision of madmen plotting to take over the world.
Are we like that?
Plotting to overthrow the young minds that face us everyday?
But the truth is,
We are those insane men rubbing our hands,
We cackle at the ideas that we have.
But can we succeed?
For in the end,
Those young minds are like the heroes of old,
Foiling the plans of the masterminds,
So that all we can say is, "Curses, foiled again".

Rain

It has been raining since before my birthday.
That was in July and this is now October.
No matter where we go there is rain.
More rain, and nothing but the rain.
How can we see anything?
How can do anything?
These rains have developed into a storm.
They are busy flooding.
We watch the television.
It was a tropical depression.
Now it is a storm named Wilma.
Poor people in Grand Cayman.
We have finished the alphabet of names,
Now we have to go Greek.
Why?
There's still a month left in the season.
So until we then we know that there will be more rain.
I wonder if we are still in the Tropics?
For it seems that we have been moved.
I wonder now what will happen?
Now that we are no longer warm.
We are cold, and there is more rain.

THE COMFORT OF CROWS

And the Devil said to God

And the Devil said to God,
"I can do everything that you can do,"
God said in reply, "Except blow breath into man".
The Devil thought these things over and said,
"I bet that I can make any one of them renounce you,"
God said, "You can try, but you won't succeed".
Then the Devil asked for one man.
God gave him Job.
The Devil lost. Well, that's how the story goes.
But I wonder if that bet is still on.
We have such evil things in this world.
We have such things that would tempt us to renounce God.
We have two priests washing dishes,
Shot through the head.
Why?
We may never understand.
But we always remember what the Devil said to God.
And, what God said to the Devil.
He can take life,
But not give it.
He can try, but he will not succeed.
We must remain strong and not renounce God.
We must remain strong in the face of all that is evil.
We must forgive those who are wicked.
We do these things,
Not for their sakes,
But for our own.
For in the end,
It is us who will be saved.
Not those who we have damned.

So whether they fly aeroplanes into buildings,
Blow up market places and squares,
We must always forgive.
The weak part of us says that we must fight back.
The strong part of us says that we must show love.
Which part will win?
Remember what the Devil said to God.
Remember what God said to the Devil.
Remember how Job showed us all.

THE COMFORT OF CROWS

A Stranger in a waiting room

While I waited for my mother to finish radiation,
I walked into the empty room.
There he sat smiling at me.
But I wondered where my aunt and cousin were.
They had gone to do a chore
So I went to the chair,
I sat there.
Then he spoke.
It was strange, for I wasn't sure at first.
Then he repeated what he said,
I had to ask him to speak slowly.
His accent was so thick.
A man from South Carolina,
With a grandmother from Tennessee.
His grandmother had been misdiagnosed.
She had cancer, they said pneumonia.
So there he was waiting for a relative,
Hoping that the treatment that my mother was undergoing,
Would be able to help his 76 year old grandmother,
Who would be undergoing chemotherapy?
So began that conversation,
Starting with the founder of the "Crips" gang on death row.
A man whose life ended when all pleas for clemency ended.
A strange thing for certain.
A strange conversation,
Then he left.
I thought, that I didn't know his name.
But we didn't have time.
Just the same, there was no way,
To know who he was.

But the thing is,
If he is out there,
He gave me something that he didn't know.
A confidence that comes,
When a woman feels appreciated.
I hope that one day I shall meet that one again.
To Say Goodbye

Beloved child, how do I tell you goodbye?
You, who were a babe in my arms?
You, who went to school?
You, who were not yet 20 years old?
It was a sudden thing that took you from us,
It was a mistake we were told,
A poor comfort that is,
When you cannot be returned.
Beloved child, lying there, with all life gone from you,
How can we stand the pain that we feel?
It was so fast that you did leave,
It was in the blink of an eye, you were gone...
There are some, who say, that they wish to be forever young and immortal,
But if this is immortality and eternal youth,
I want it not.
I would rather hear your voice and see your smile.
Your spirit flew quickly like a dove.
How can we say goodbye?
Beloved, precious sweet child,
We must and so we say, goodbye...
So go to sleep now darling boy,
And rest eternally with the Father.

THE COMFORT OF CROWS

(Shaun McClue Jan. 27, 1986 – Jan. 18, 2006)

Waiting for the shoe to drop

How often do we expect things to happen?
Then they don't.
How often do we plan and pray for a better tomorrow?
And it comes up worse.
What more is there to left to happen?
I expect it will be worse.
The depression that eats at the soul.
It comes and it goes.
There are things that happen to try and wipe it away.
But those things are so far in between.
Still it returns.
The demands.
The questions.
The pleas.
It keeps pounding like a drum.
The madness that seems to lurk.
It lurks just behind the eyes.
It wants to prey on the mind.
It at times is kept at bay.
But alone in the world of thoughts.
No one to keep those things away.
No soldier to help shore up the barricades.
The hollow sound is deafening.
No one notices.
No one sees.
No one cares.
It is over.

It is ending.

Waiting and praying.
Praying and waiting.
The other shoe will drop.
Shatter like the glass on the floor.
Cinderella out the door.
She takes her mop.
The cinders are calling.
The blood is dripping.
The way is hollow.
The stench follows.
Waiting and praying.
Praying and waiting.
The other shoe must drop.
It is dangling by the hair.
The sword that will cut.
The knife that will wound.
It is over.
It is ending.
(April 6, 2007)

THE COMFORT OF CROWS

Rain in a Caribbean Country

Large fat drops of ice cold water
Running with mud down potholed streets
People running for they have no umbrellas
'Carry Umbrella? What fa'? It soon done.'
Heavy streams of water battle the cars
As each is determined to have the road
The culverts overflow as the sewer bubbles
For the water has nowhere to go
Men riding motorbikes stand while they
Navigate the streets, whose holes are filled
With murky water designed to trap
The unaware fish driving the fancy car
As suddenly it starts,
It stops.
People continue
Jumping
Hopping
Skipping
Living

(May 2008)

Tears (For RevVee)

What tears can fall from my eyes
That can show how much you matter?
How much rain can stream from the skies
To let you know that you are missed?
We spend so much time trying
We spend so much time crying

Every second we tried
Every hour we cried
Did you know that we loved you?
Did we tell you often enough?
Were we loud enough for you to hear?
Did you understand that we truly cared?
What measure of tears can there be?
The sun is no longer bright
The birds are quiet in the trees
The air is cold now that you are gone.
Your laughter and promise
We hold on to
Your voice filled with patience and wisdom
We cherish dearly
Darling friend
Be at peace
You suffer no more
Continue to watch over us
Until we meet
Again.

THE COMFORT OF CROWS

Monday Morning

It's after 7
And the people are on their way to work
There are a lot of people
Making their way
Men with large scandal bags
Walking to work
Women in jeans and flip flops
The women who work in offices
Leading their uniformed young to the school on the way.
Cars are increasing as the hour passes
Several refuse to obey the traffic signals
While policemen lean against their car
Laughing before they have to start writing tickets.
Taxi – men stop obstructing traffic
As a policeman on a motorbike scowls at them.
The square is littered with bright red stalls
That look like large metal mailboxes
The midday sun will turn those into a furnace.
Cars are turning into the schools
To release the students or rather to burden the schools
While the homeless man sits on the sidewalk.
Through the main square
School girls of all kinds walk.
Their hair pulled into various styles
While their book bags are empty.
They chatter as they walk and it is obvious that they
Have no intention to learn.
The schoolyard is noisy.
The cackling barnyard is filled with the empty barrels.
There is an attempt at getting them to be silent

But like everything else
It fails.
Monday morning
The start of the week, again.
March 30,2009.

What if she had said 'no'?

What if she had said 'no'?
Told the angel Gabriel
'I said no. Now please go.'
Where would we be?
If she had said 'no'.
Would a Christ child have been born?
In that lowly manger
On that wintry morn?
Who would have gone for you and me
All the way to Calvary?
Or would it be some other girl?
Some virgin born
Who would have taken
That long walk
From Pilate's court
To that lonely hill where the criminals are slain (crucified)?
Would there be some other name
That generations would call and say
Blessed is she
Who opened her heart
Blessed is she
Who bore the child
Where would we be?
If she had said 'no'

THE COMFORT OF CROWS

She would not have suffered
To see her child
Who she carried
Who was still innocent
Walk with the shame of the cross
Whipped, bleeding and crucified
If she had known
Would she have said 'yes'
To love the child and know
He was born to save all Mankind
He was born to light the way
His path was torture and pain
A burden He carried
A burden she bore
Knowing this,
Would she have said,
'I am the servant of the Lord,
Let it be done to me as you have said.'
December 2, 2010

Gentle Jesus

Gentle Jesus, meek and mild
Look upon your little child
Though flawed and sinful
Everyday, please just love me
All the same
Gentle Jesus, meek and mild
Here stands your little child
Help me resist all the ways
That tempt good people from your
Path to stray
Gentle Jesus, meek and mild
Do not turn away from your child
Though there are times I may run away
Please remember that I am not a saint
Gentle Jesus, meek and mild
Do not be angry with your little child
Though I am not the fruitful tree
Do not be angry with me
Gentle Jesus, meek and mild
Life is hard for your little child
Keep me close to you always
So that my steps may follow yours
All the way.
(Jan 5 2011)

THE COMFORT OF CROWS

Grandfather has died

I hate when the phone rings
Early in the morning.
It is always the bearer of
Bad things.
True, it may be a wrong
Number
But more often that not
It is Bad News.
The phone rang at 5:34 a.m.
It was my uncle
He said that my grandfather
Was dead.
My father answered the phone
I refused to pick up
I knew it was bad
Did not want to hear.
Strangely there were no tears
We shed them a little over
A year ago.
When the doctors said
Prepare.
My mother has been waiting since
February last year
For the call that finally came.
Mr. Munchun
Has passed on and is now ready
For the grave.
Phone calls were made
All over the island
And also

To those in North America
U.S.A. and Canada.
Grandfather and father, papa
Has died.
No one cried because the
Tears were spent
We were prepared.
There is no gaping void
No hole to fill.
He knew he was loved
We knew he loved
All things are finished.
A fulfilled life
And now, he, the last of his
Generation has gone on.
Farmer, husband, father and grandfather
How many great grandchildren
Have good memories?
The ones in our family do.
A man he was
Imperfect
But he loved
For us, that is more than enough.
(June 12, 2012.)

THE COMFORT OF CROWS

I Broke A Nail

I broke a nail,
And didn't lose a shoe,
Neither a horse nor rider too;
I broke a nail,
And the world suffered,
Battles were won and kingdoms lost.
I broke a nail,
And Susan rolled in her grave,
As iron jawed angels were marched off to jail.
I broke a nail,
And no one solved the mystery of life,
There was still civil strife.
I broke a nail,
And the world went on,
People were killed and others were born.
I broke a nail,
And no one stood still,
Every cup was still full to the brim.
I broke a nail,
And a star was born,
As another faded from sight into the dark and cold night.
I broke a nail,
The world still turned,
There were still people who yearned.
I broke a nail,
And new songs were written,
While the old ones still played on the radio.
I broke a nail,
And my favourite show was cancelled,
While my cat slept on my pillow.

There is no bugle call,
There is no lightning flash,
There is only the loud roll of thunder.
Somewhere coups are being plotted,
Children are playing recitals,
And students are cramming for an exam.
All these things are happening.
A woman sings of love and time,
And I broke a nail.

THE COMFORT OF CROWS

My Mother

Little Indian woman hanging out the clothes,
on the line in the sun,
like her mother before.
The laundry being carefully arranged
so as to maximise the day's rays.
On that line
that stretches back in time
telling the history of family
and riches lost in the annals of mist.
How far back does that line of clothes go?
Back to my grandmother
the first born of her parents?
We still wonder if she was born here or in India.
She says she was a small child on the boat,
(our family they say came after the indentured
and thus were not enslaved, for indenture was simply slavery disguised,
shh!)
My grandfather, her husband was born here, but India was always
nearby, but, we are following that clothesline.
Through the port of Calcutta,
yes, it was called a blackhole too.
From there to Bihar, the villages
of Punjab and Sunab
places now long gone.
Stretching back in time to Persia,
but that is too far,
(shh! secrets!)
Coming back along the line,
following the boat's wake
across the Atlantic

this too was a middle passage
(shh! don't tell the others, they will say you lie.)
Coming into St. Mary
in search of a home,
there was that one uncle, as I was told,
had a large nugget of gold,
knew he'd be cheated by white English man
so made friends with the descendants of freed Africans.
Help him, he claimed to make a better sale,
help him they did in their own way
cut his throat and left him to die,
family found him under the bridge
no gold in sight ... (shh! don't talk secrets that would show the hatred
the resentment and prejudice. They always feel justified in their name
calling,
after all even though our country conquered and pillaged too and we
cursed that
we skin black and our mothers, sisters, daughters, aunts and cousins
raped too .... shh!)
Following that line of clothes
blowing in the wind
from Coolietown down to Port Maria
and my grandfather, great – grandfather and mother too.
Hindu priest my aunt Myrtle says
did his prayers and found his zen.
Songs I heard later and felt the resonance in them, but that is other story
time.
This is my mother,
born from this union of Beatrice and Aubrey
the seventh child of nine,
my mother swears my grandmother had two per year,
but there was trouble

THE COMFORT OF CROWS

always is with poverty
(shh! why you not shutting up here?)
A great – grandfather who gambled away his land
leaving a son struggling
anxious not knowing what to do,
the poor man broke
sent to Bellevue (shush! you don't hear these things can't happen to us,
we not human, we Indian)
My mother never forgave him seeing her mother suffer as a child.
Could not forgive him
until me her child,
broke in two
nearly dying
and sent her searching
to the internet, where
celebrities explained
Clinical depression and anxiety they named.
Hereditary it is with clues in the blood,
there was the cousin, who could not take this hell
doused himself in kerosene oil, lit himself on fire
for there was no help, and so he chose death instead.
These things my mother now understood,
She could let go her grudge
forgive her father,
grow close to him
and love him like her mother.
She came to Kingston,
endured a hard working life ...
made mistakes (shh! don't talk 'bout the man she made you with.)
Married my father (my daddy who raised me)
Worked hard to own a home
pushed and nagged to get her two children educated.

Became ill but struggled
until she was forced to retire
but all through this
her children were clean
wearing the clothes she hung in the sun.
Little Indian woman hanging out the clothes
like all the others who came before,
until it comes down to me
half – Indian woman hanging out the clothes
looking at the line of history.
(December 28, 2023.)

THE COMFORT OF CROWS

Barefoot Island Girl
I long to be that
Barefoot Island girl,
That I used to be,
Before life and people, beat me down.
Running carefree on the beach,
Diving into the cool sea,
The rolling waves
Cradling me.
Those days of swimwear,
One piece
Bikini
Shirt and shorts
Sinking toes into the sand
While the white foam
On the clear water
Moved to and fro.
Hellshire beach,
Eating fried fish and festival,
Drinking cold coconut water
Right from the nut itself.
Swimming at Ochie,
Then the beaches of Negril,
Watching white tourists
Burn red.
In Negril was the scandal,
The topless white woman,
But we shrugged it off
After all we had budding beasts.
Nights playing dominos,
Board games,
Family time and vacation,

Simple times
Now, I travel on the new highway,
My parents aged passengers,
Going to Ochie to meet,
The cousins from foreign climes.
Family meetings and younger folk
The cousins
They discuss the days of old
While we sit on a balcony by the sea.
We traverse the sand
My mother holding my arm,
I have to take of my shoes,
Sinking into those sand dunes.
The new cousin Charlene
Is with us too,
As we go in search
To buy some food.
Rain showers pelt
As we head back,
Light rains
Sandy feet.
As I walk through the
People hotel,
I sense that barefoot island girl
Raise her head.
The confidence and strength
That was lost
Is still there
A warm feeling to behold.
That barefoot island girl
Reminds me
That I must have the courage

THE COMFORT OF CROWS

To live free.
June 18, 2024.

About the Author

About the Author

Denise Neita-Chen has spent the last 29 years of her life in a classroom. She also has been creating stories since she was 6 years old and invented an entire life history to explain her aunt, who she thought was her cousin. Having tried and failed to make a living as a writer, she continues to try to change people's minds about life and literature from her chalkboard.